NATURAL WORLD

GIANT
PANDA

HABITATS • LIFE CYCLES • FOOD CHAINS • THREATS

Malcolm Penny

RSVP

**RAINTREE
STECK-VAUGHN**
PUBLISHERS
A Steck-Vaughn Company

Austin, Texas
www.steck-vaughn.com

NATURAL WORLD

Chimpanzee • Crocodile • Dolphin • Elephant • Giant Panda
Great White Shark • Killer Whale • Lion • Orangutan
Penguin • Polar Bear • Tiger

Cover: Face to face with a giant panda
Title page: Bamboo is the panda's main food.
Contents page: A young panda clings to a branch.
Index page: A panda enjoys a light snack.

Published by Raintree Steck-Vaughn Publishers, an imprint of Steck-Vaughn Company

Library of Congress Cataloging-in-Publication Data
Penny, Malcolm.
Giant panda / Malcolm Penny.
    p.   cm.—(Natural world)
    Includes bibliographical references and index.
    Summary: Describes the habits and behavior of giant pandas at different stages of their lives, as well as threats to their continued survival.
    ISBN 0-7398-1063-4 (hard)
    0-7398-2028-1 (soft)
    1.Giant panda—Juvenile literature.
    [1. Giant panda. 2. Pandas.]
    I. Title. II. Series.
    QL737.C214P45   2000
    599.789—dc21   99-43257

Printed in Italy. Bound in the United States.
1 2 3 4 5 6 7 8 9 0 04 03 02 01 00

Picture acknowledgments
Bruce Coleman Collection 9 (Sophy & Michael Day), 11 (Rod Williams), 14 (Clive Hicks), 15 (Gerald S. Cubitt), 16 (Rod Williams), 18 (Hans Reinhard), 23 (Sophy & Michael Day), 27, 30 (Hans Reinhard), 31 (Hans Reinhard), 35 (Sophy & Michael Day), 37 (Mark Carwardine), 42 (Hans Reinhard), 45 middle (Sophy & Michael Day), 45 bottom (Hans Reinhard), 48 (Erwin & Peggy Bauer); Heather Angel/Biofotos 1, 3, 6, 7, 10, 12–13, 13, 17, 20, 21, 22, 24, 25, 26, 28, 29, 32, 33, 34, 38, 39, 40, 41, 44 top, 44 bottom, 45 top; Still Pictures 8 (Roland Seitre), 36 (Roland Seitre), 43 (Roland Seitre), 44 middle (Roland Seitre); Tony Stone Images *front cover* (Keren Su).
Maps on page 4 by Victoria Webb and Peter Bull.
All other artwork by Michael Posen.

Contents

Meet the Giant Panda

The giant panda is one of the most popular and easily recognized mammals in the world. Sadly, it also one of the rarest. This large, shy, stocky creature is a black-and-white relative of bears.

The giant panda is in great danger of becoming extinct. It is found in the wild in just three provinces of China—Sichuan, Shaanxi, and Gansu.

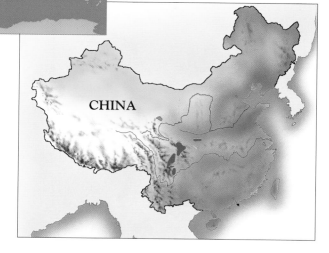

◀ China's position in the world

CHINA

▲ The red areas on this map show where giant pandas live in the wild.

PANDA FACTS

The giant panda's Latin name, *Ailuropoda melanoleuca*, means "cat-footed black and white."

●

A giant panda measures 28 to 30 in. (70–80 cm) tall at the shoulder when on all four legs, and 66 in. (170 cm) when standing upright. It weighs 220 to 330 lbs. (100–150 kg). Males are usually about 10 percent larger than females.

▶ An adult giant panda

Front paws
The wrist bone of each front paw is enlarged to form a "false thumb." The panda grips bamboo by pressing the first two claws against its false thumb.

Head
The panda's skull is very heavy. The powerful chewing muscles that operate the jaws are anchored to the cheekbones.

Eyes
The panda's sensitive eyes, with their vertical pupils, give it good night vision.

Legs
Sturdy legs carry the weight of the panda's heavy body.

Teeth
The giant panda has no shearing or incisor teeth for slicing through flesh. Most of its teeth are molars, which are broad to grind up food such as tough bamboo stems. It also has large canine teeth, with which it can defend itself.

Feet
Pads at the base of the claws (see above) improve the panda's grip. The feet are covered with thick hair, which helps the panda walk over snow and ice.

5

The Panda's Habitat

The giant panda lives in China's remote mountain forests, 8,500 ft. to 11,500 ft. (2,600 to 3,500 m) above sea level, where the mountain air is very thin. Some scientists think that the panda's blood is specially adapted to carry extra oxygen, so that it can survive at these high altitudes.

At the upper levels of the forests, tall conifer trees grow among rhododendrons and scattered clumps of short, slender bamboo. Lower down the mountain slopes, where the forest is thicker, dense clumps of bamboo up to 10 ft. (3 m) tall are found between the mixture of conifers and deciduous trees.

▶ In the mountains of China, the temperature rarely rises above 68° F (20° C), and in winter it can fall to as low as 19° F (−7° C).

▲ The giant panda shares its cold, misty habitat with many other forest animals, including red pandas.

RED PANDAS

The red panda is a smaller, more nimble animal than the giant panda, and a better climber. Like the panda, it has a false thumb. Its teeth are similar to those of the giant panda, and it may also have specially adapted blood. Despite this, most scientists now agree that the two species are not closely related. The giant panda is a bear, while the red panda is related to raccoons. The similarities between the two types of pandas occur because both animals are bamboo-eaters that live at high altitude.

A Panda Is Born

Female pandas breed every two or three years. After mating, a female panda is pregnant for from 96 to 168 days. She looks for a place to make a den where she can give birth, such as at the base of a large, hollow tree. Then she lines it with leafy branches and clumps of vegetation.

A panda mother is about 900 times heavier than her newborn cub, which weighs less than 5 oz. (142 g). At birth, the cub is about the size of a rat. It is pink, blind, and completely helpless.

▲ Newborn giant panda cubs in a breeding center in China. One of these cubs died at five days old, but her brother (above) survived. In the top photo he is ten days old.

ADOPTED CUBS?

Very occasionally, wild pandas have been seen with two cubs. Some scientists suggest that it happens when a mother adopts a stray cub whose own mother has died. Others think it occurs when a mother tries to raise both her twin cubs.

Giant pandas usually have one or two cubs, or very rarely three. The mother will almost always rear one of her cubs and ignore any others, which soon die. That is probably because a newborn cub needs constant attention during the first few weeks of life. It wiggles actively when it is fed and has to be held firmly by its mother.

▼ A mother cleans her ten-week-old cub in a breeding center in China.

Early Days

For the first week of its life, a giant panda cub is fed by its mother every hour. The cub sucks milk from its mother's teats. When feeding is over, the mother then spends about fifteen minutes licking the cub clean. The mother cradles her cub with her forepaws most of the first three weeks.

While it is small, the cub is in great danger from a wide range of predators, including stoats, weasels, martens, golden cats, and leopards. After two weeks, the cub looks rather like a piglet, but the pattern of its fur is beginning to show.

▲ A mother cleans her six-month-old cub's fur.

▶ China's mountain forests are also home to the beautiful golden cat, which is a serious threat to baby pandas.

Development and Danger

A giant panda cub develops very slowly. It does not open its eyes for the first six or eight weeks, and cannot crawl until it is two-and-a-half or three months. By the age of four months, when it weighs about 9 lbs. (4 kg), the cub can walk on its own.

After about eight months, the cub is weaned and starts to eat its first stems of bamboo. The cub may become infested by parasitic worms, such as roundworms, which are found in food and in the soil. The worms live inside the panda's gut and can make it very sick. They may even cause it to die.

▼ At first, panda cubs are very vulnerable. By the time they are about a year old, like this cub, they can defend themselves against all but the largest predators.

The cub can now defend itself against small predators, such as stoats and weasels, using its sharp claws and large canine teeth. If bigger predators threaten, it climbs quickly into a tree to escape.

▲ Young pandas are good climbers and will scramble up the nearest tree trunk if they sense danger approaching.

13

Growing Up

The cub normally stays with its mother until it is at least eighteen months old, and sometimes for three years or more. It follows its mother through the forest, learning from her where to find the best food plants at different times of the year.

▲ A panda nestles in a clump of bamboo. Different kinds of bamboo are good to eat at different times of the year.

One of the first things the panda cub learns about forest life is not to waste valuable energy struggling up and down steep slopes through dense undergrowth. Pandas usually walk along gentle, well-trodden paths made by deer and other forest animals.

Other Forest Dwellers

As it gets to know the forest, the young panda meets red pandas and many other animals, including tragopan and monal pheasants. These birds are brightly colored to enable them to find each other in the gloomy forest.

▼ Tragopans are one of nine species of colorful pheasants that can be found in the forests of China.

Troops of golden monkeys live in the treetops. They have thick, shining coats and blue faces. On the forest floor are porcupines and musk deer. Musk deer have no antlers but defend themselves with long, tusk-like teeth that protrude from their upper lips.

But danger lurks in the depths of the forest, too. Young cubs must watch out for large predators. Leopards will sometimes prey on panda cubs, but dholes are the cub's worst natural enemy. Dholes are hunting dogs that live in packs of between five to twelve animals. They have been known to kill and eat old pandas as well as young cubs.

▲ A male musk deer has visible tusks. The female's tusks do not show outside her mouth.

MUSK DEER

Musk deer are often hunted for their scent glands. The oily liquid from the gland is used in traditional Chinese medicine to treat a wide range of diseases, and also in the West to make expensive perfumes. To collect 2 lbs. (1 kg) of the liquid, which can sell for more than $47,000, about 70 deer have to be killed.

A female golden ▶
snub-nosed monkey
with her baby. Males
sometimes leap down
from the trees from as
high as 100 ft. (30 m),
breaking branches as
they fall to the ground.

17

Food and Feeding

Like its mother, the young panda is soon eating mainly arrow bamboo, which grows on the lower slopes of the mountain. Pandas wander from clump to clump, selecting a few shoots here and there. They often smell them carefully before they eat them, which may help them decide which are the best shoots to eat.

▼ No one is sure why pandas spend so much time deciding which shoots to eat.

A panda may sit feeding for an hour in one place, or wander to a new feeding spot after a few minutes.

18

GIANT PANDA FOOD CHAIN

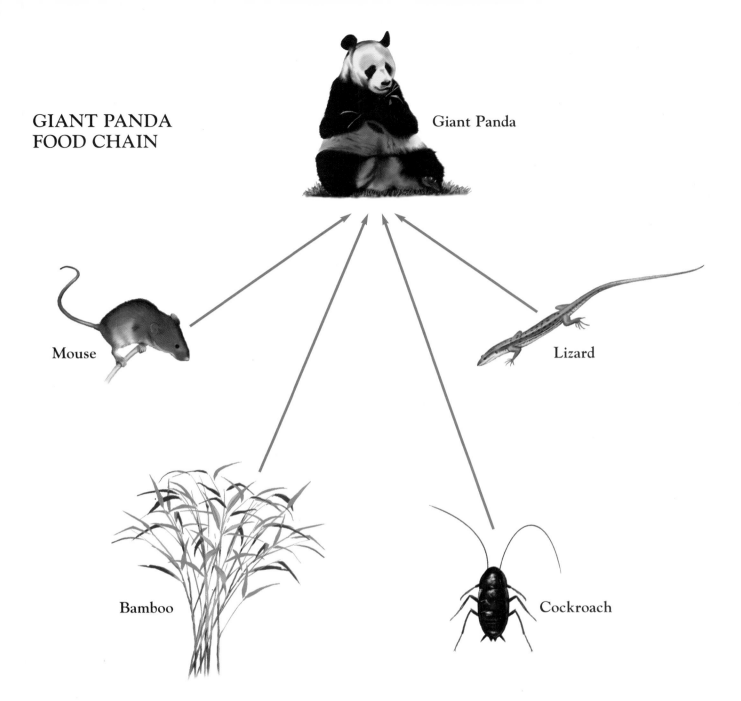

Giant Panda

Mouse

Lizard

Bamboo

Cockroach

▲ Adult giant pandas are at the top of their food chain. Pandas sometimes eat things other than bamboo, including insects and small rodents and reptiles.

Umbrella bamboo is a panda delicacy that grows new shoots in May and June. The pandas specially seek out this type of bamboo. They eat only the plant's soft shoots and avoid the tougher leaves. Some other animals avoid the leaves, too, which suggests that they may be difficult to digest, or even poisonous at this time of year.

How Pandas Eat

When a giant panda feeds, it sits up on its
haunches and lifts the bamboo to its mouth with
one forepaw. It chews leaves and shoots very
carefully, but only roughly crunches up the stems,
so that its droppings afterward contain a mass of
splinters. The panda's gut has a tough lining to
protect it against swallowed splinters.

Arrow bamboo is easy to eat. The panda holds
the stem in one paw and bites pieces off, just as
we might eat a stick of celery. However, umbrella
bamboo is not so easy, because its shoots have a
tough, bristly outer casing, which the panda
strips off with its teeth before eating the shoot.

▲ A panda's false
thumb helps it grip the
slender bamboo stems
firmly as it eats.

Bamboo is plentiful in the forest, but it is low in energy-giving carbohydrates, so an adult giant panda must eat a vast amount to get the energy it needs. An adult panda will consume about 650 shoots a day, weighing about 85 lbs. (38 kg) —a quarter of its own body weight.

▼ This giant panda is using its tongue to strip the leaves off a bamboo shoot.

When the Bamboo Flowers

Bamboo is a type of grass. Like other grasses, it dies once it has flowered and produced seeds. Some small bamboo species flower every year, but larger species may have a flowering cycle of up to 120 years.

Arrow bamboo, the panda's main source of food, flowers every forty to fifty years. When flowering takes place, it can be a disaster for the pandas. As soon as the bamboo plants in a particular area have seeded, they all die off at once, leaving the pandas with nothing to eat.

▼ A panda carefully chews up bamboo leaves, including their stems, before swallowing them.

To avoid starving to death, the pandas must move to a place where there is enough food to keep them alive until new bamboo shoots appear. They either travel to parts of the mountain where the arrow bamboo has not yet flowered, or to the valleys, where different species of bamboo grow.

Pandas that are too old or sick to make the journey will die, but the rest will survive.

▲ When the bamboo flowers and goes to seed, it is a time of feasting for many seed-eating animals. But pandas risk starvation, and they may have to travel long distances in search of food.

23

▲ Pandas sometimes eat tree bark. The bark may contain vitamins that are not found in other kinds of food.

Other Food

Although pandas eat mainly bamboo, they will sometimes feed on bulbs, herbs, tree bark, and even meat. Pandas do catch and eat large insects and small rodents and reptiles. There are even reports of a panda catching fish.

Panda droppings have also been found containing the bones of golden monkeys and musk deer. But it is unlikely that a heavy panda could have chased and caught these nimble animals. The panda probably found them when they were already dead.

Poachers and scientists sometimes use smoked meat to lure pandas into traps. This may be more a sign of the panda's curiosity about strange scents in the forest than its taste for such food.

Pandas get most of the water they need from their diet of juicy bamboo shoots. They sometimes make a drinking pool for themselves by digging a hole by a stream and waiting for it to fill with water.

▼ Although pandas usually get their water by eating bamboo, they may also lick snow to increase their intake of water.

◀ Pandas make a variety of different sounds to communicate with each other. Low, growling notes travel farthest through the thick forest.

Communication

The young panda must learn how to communicate with other pandas. Although they are usually silent, pandas have a wide range of calls for special occasions. A small cub cries like a human baby, with a high-pitched call that is impossible for a parent to ignore.

During the breeding season, a female stands on a high ridge and produces deep roars, barks, and moans that can be heard in neighboring valleys. When she is ready to mate, she utters a strange bleating call, rather like a goat.

Pandas also communicate with each other with their body scent and strong-smelling urine, which they use to mark the areas where they live.

▶ Unlike the rest of the bear family, pandas do not use facial expressions to communicate. When one panda wants to threaten another, it simply stares at its rival with its head down, perhaps so that its black ears look like another pair of eyes against the white fur of its neck.

A Giant Panda's Day

Since they live in forests on steep hillsides, giant pandas are very hard to study. By fitting them with special collars that give off radio signals, scientists have been able to find out what they do and where they go, and what a typical day in the life of a panda is like.

For most of its waking hours, a panda moves between clumps of bamboo looking for food. It feeds both day and night, but is most active in the early morning and late afternoon. Pandas normally rest for from two to four hours between meals, but in summer they rest for longer, sometimes sleeping for six hours or more.

▼ Pandas can sometimes be seen rolling down slopes. It is possible that this is just a playful act, but it may have a more practical use, such as to dislodge twigs from their fur.

▲ This panda is resting with its head propped on a tree root, to keep it away from the freezing ground.

With its thick, oily coat, a panda has little need to seek shelter, except in the heaviest rain, when it might retreat into a hollow tree or a cave. The panda rarely grooms its fur, but keeps it in good condition by rolling on the ground and rubbing soil into its belly with its paws. The soil absorbs grease and grime on the fur. When the soil dries and falls off, it takes the grease and grime with it.

To avoid losing vital body heat to the cold ground, the panda usually sleeps lying on a thick patch of pine needles. It loses most heat through its head, so it rests its head on its hind legs or against the roots of a tree.

Leaving Home

Giant pandas are fully grown by the time they are three years old. By now, most pandas are completely independent. A panda's first task as an adult is to find an area of its own, where it can feed undisturbed by others.

Each adult lives in an area of 1.5 to 2.5 sq. mi. (4 to 6 sq. km), known as its home range. Within this is a patch measuring less than one fifth of a square mile (0.5 sq. km), which is the panda's actual home. This is called its core area.

Adult females stay close to their core areas, but males roam widely through their home range to see what other pandas live nearby. This helps them learn where to find the females when it is time to breed, and where their male rivals are.

▶ The best core areas have gentle slopes with a thick cover of bamboo. Older pandas usually have the best spots, so young adults have to make do with steeper slopes with less bamboo. When the older pandas die, younger ones may be able to move into their core areas.

◀ A male panda explores his home range, looking for a female with whom to breed.

Scent-marking

Unlike many other animals, a panda does not physically defend a territory by fighting. Instead, it uses its body scent to let other pandas know when they are entering its home range or coming close to its core area.

A panda marks the boundaries of its home range and core area by rubbing the scent glands under its tail over bushes and trees. Some trees are rubbed smooth and stained by many years of use. A male may walk backward up a tree until he is doing a handstand, to make the scent mark as high up as possible.

▲ A male panda rubs his scent gland on a rock. The scent mark will let other pandas know that they are in his territory.

Strong-smelling urine sprayed on tree trunks and rocks is also used as a boundary marker, as are scratches on tree bark. All these things will tell a panda exploring a new area that other pandas are around, even if it does not see them.

► Even on small trees, scratch marks, sometimes very deep, are a message to other pandas.

PANDA MARKINGS

Some scientists have suggested that pandas' striking black-and-white markings enable then to see each other from afar, and avoid meetings that might result in fights.

Mating

Females are ready to breed when they are four or five years old, and males at six or seven. A female tells nearby males that she is ready to mate by calling, and probably also through changes in the smell of her scent and urine.

Males compete with each other to be her mate. This can lead to fighting, which is otherwise very rare among pandas. Males do not usually fight with their claws and teeth, but shove and bump each other in trials of strength. The fight stops when one contestant realizes that he cannot win.

▲ This wrestling match may be play, or it may have a more serious purpose. A fight for the right to mate with a female usually takes the form of bumping and shoving.

The winning male tries to mate with the female. If the female does not run away, she will attack him until she decides that it is the right moment for mating. After mating, other males may then mate with her.

Mating with several males gives the female a better chance of becoming pregnant. It will also help to protect her cub. A male panda will occasionally kill a cub so that its mother will need to breed again, giving him the chance to mate with her. However, males do not kill their own cubs. If a female mates with several males, the males are unlikely to kill the cubs that she gives birth to.

▼ A male panda (right) mates with a female (left) after winning a fight with a rival male.

Threats

Since giant pandas are so hard to study in the wild, it is not certain how many of them are left. But researchers estimate that there are probably only between 800 and 1,100 giant pandas living in the wild today in China.

The greatest threat to pandas' survival comes from hunters. Pandas are sometimes killed for their coats, which are used as rugs. Giant pandas are easy to hunt, because they are slow-moving and easy to spot in the forest.

◄ Skins of wild animals on sale in a market in Sichuan province, China. Many pandas are illegally killed for their fur each year.

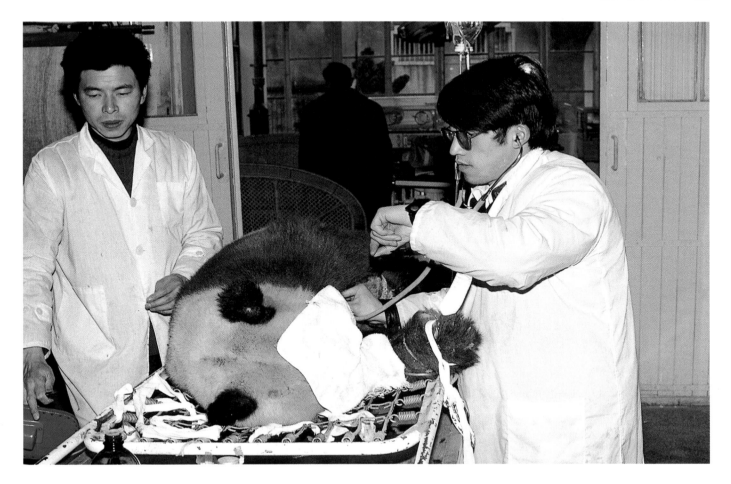

In 1987, the Chinese government introduced strict laws to protect the pandas. There are severe punishments for anyone who kills pandas or who is caught selling panda skins. But the skins are so valuable that some hunters are still prepared to take the risk.

▲ These Chinese scientists are measuring a panda's pulse rate. Pandas are often injured by the snares set by hunters of deer and bears.

Other pandas are accidentally killed by hunters who are trying to catch musk deer and Asiatic black bears. Pandas occasionally walk into the snares that the hunters set up on forest paths. They often die before they can be released.

Deforestation

Giant pandas need big, old trees for dens where they can produce cubs, so they need old, undisturbed forests with good growths of bamboo. But the pandas' home is disappearing fast. China has a billion people to feed and house, and there is constant pressure to cut down forests to create new farmland and to provide firewood and timber for building.

Pandas also need to be able to move to new parts of the forest to find food when the bamboo in one area dies off. Today, these journeys are no longer possible because so much of the forest has been cut down. In 1983, at least eighty pandas starved to death after the bamboo died off in the Qionglai mountain reserve.

▲ The pandas' misty forest home is under threat from the spread of human settlements and farming.

▶ Protecting the panda's forest home will help save many other rare plants and animals, as well as the pandas themselves.

Saving Giant Pandas

There are thirty-four giant panda preserves in China, where the pandas' forest home is protected. Together, they cover an area of more than 3,800 sq. mi. (10,000 sq. km). The largest reserve is at Wolong, in the mountains of eastern Sichuan. Although it has been protected since 1975, the preserve had still lost half its pandas to poachers by 1986. Despite this, the Chinese government is determined to make the preserve a success.

▼ Wolong's scientific station is the center of Chinese panda research.

▲ A panda from the Wolong breeding center climbs into its cage to go home after an outing in the forest.

One plan is to create "corridors" of protected forest between the preserves. This would make it easier for the pandas to move from one preserve to another, and enable them to reach new feeding grounds when the bamboo dies off. It would also improve their chances of breeding successfully in the wild, because it would be a way of mixing males and females from different areas.

41

▲ Pandas always draw big crowds in zoos throughout the world.

Pandas in Zoos

To help the pandas survive, many zoos are trying to breed pandas. The first giant panda born in captivity was Ming Ming, in Beijing Zoo, China, in 1963, followed by two more in the next two years. It seemed to be the start of a great breakthrough in the battle to save the panda from extinction, but this has not proved to be the case.

A FUTURE IN THE WILD?

Pandas born in zoos will not be released into their natural habitats until the problems that the wild pandas face have been solved. The future of the giant panda depends on the protection of the wild panda population, and its home in China's mountain forests.

Outside China, the zoos most successful at breeding pandas have been Mexico City, with four cubs that survived infancy, and Japan's Tokyo Zoo, which raised two cubs. Other zoos have had some successes, but the cubs are often stillborn, or die within the first few days. Scientists are trying to discover why it is so hard to breed pandas in captivity.

On page 47 you will find the address of the World Wide Fund for Nature, which is working to save the giant panda.

▼ A mother and her young cub in the breeding center at Chengdu, China

Panda Life Cycle

 **1** At birth, giant panda cubs are the size of rats. They are pink, blind, and completely helpless. Female giant pandas may have two or three cubs, but usually only one will survive.

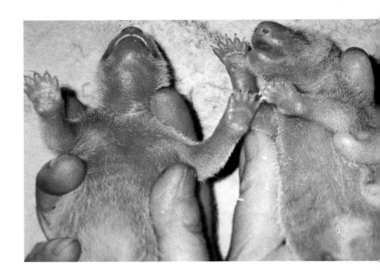

 **2** During the first three weeks, the cub stays cradled in its mother's forepaws. After about six or eight weeks it opens its eyes, and at two-and-a-half or three months, the cub can crawl.

 **3** At four months, the panda cub can walk on its own, but it will not be weaned until it is at least eight months old.

 The cub stays with its mother until it is eighteen months old, and sometimes for three years or more. By three years of age, it will have reached its full adult size and weight and will be completely independent.

 Female giant pandas are ready to breed at four or five years old, and males at six or seven.

 In captivity, giant pandas can live for thirty years, but in the wild they only live for up to twenty years.

Glossary

Canine teeth Long, pointed teeth toward the front of a giant panda's jaws, two on the top jaw and two on the bottom jaw.

Core area The place where a giant panda makes its home.

Extinct No longer existing.

False thumb A giant panda's extended wrist bone, which helps it grip bamboo.

Home range A panda's feeding ground.

Incisor teeth Sharp teeth for cutting through flesh.

Mammal An animal that feeds its young on milk produced by the female's mammary glands.

Molars Broad teeth for grinding up food.

Parasitic worm A worm that lodges in the gut of an animal and feeds off it.

Poachers People who hunt and kill animals illegally.

Predators Animals that kill other creatures for food.

Pregnant A female animal is pregnant when a baby is developing in her womb.

Reserve A place where animals and wildlife are protected.

Scent gland A part of a panda's body that produces a strong-smelling liquid, which serves as a signal to other pandas.

Snares Traps for catching animals. A snare consists of a loop of wire or cord that tightens around part of an animal's body, preventing it from escaping.

Stillborn Dead at birth.

Territory The area in which an animal, or group of animals, lives, and which it defends against intruders and enemies.

Weaned A young animal has been weaned when it stops drinking its mother's milk.

Further Information

Organizations to Contact

Center for Environmental Education
1725 DeSales Street NW
Suite 500
Washington, DC 20036

Friends of the Earth (U.S.A.)
218 D Street SE
Washington, DC 20003

Greenpeace U.S.A.
1436 U Street NW
Washington, DC 20009

Nature Conservancy
1815 N. Lynn Street
Arlington, VA 22209

World Wildlife Fund
1250 24th Street NW
Washington, DC 20037

Websites

WWF Panda Site
www.panda.org
Everything You Need to Know About the Giant
Panda

www.fonz.org/ppage.htm
Run by the Friends of the National Zoo in
Washington DC. Information, a game, and an
animated map charting the panda's decline.

The Bear Den
www.nature-net.com/bears/
polar.html
This site has information and pictures of polar
bears and links to sites about other bears.

Books to Read

Brown, Gary. *The Great Bear Almanac*. New York:
Lyons & Burford, 1993.

Herrero, Steven. *Bear Attacks: Their Causes and
Avoidance*. New York: Nick Lyons Books, 1985.

Lynch, Wayne. *Bears*. Vancouver: Douglas &
McIntyre, 1993.

Pollack, Steve. *Atlas of Endangered Animals*. New
York: Facts on File, 1993.

Stirling, Ian, ed. *Bears: Majestic Creatures of the
Wild*. New York: Rodale Press, 1993.

Index

All the numbers in **bold** refer to photographs or illustrations.